"A day without laughter is a day wasted."

– Charlie Chaplin

The Ultimate Dirty Jokes for Adults

777 Inappropriate Jokes!

Table of Contents:

Introduction: Buckle Up, Buttercup! 4

Chapter 1: Office Shenanigans 7

Chapter 2: Office Shenanigans – The After-Hours Edition! ... 14

Chapter 3: Relationships – Love, Lust, and Everything In Between 21

Chapter 4: Relationships – Love, Lust, and Everything In Between (Extra Dirty Edition) 28

Chapter 5: Bar Banter – Drinks, Laughs, and Inappropriate Shenanigans 35

Chapter 6: Bar Banter – Where the Drinks Flow and Standards Lower 42

Chapter 7: Around the Bedroom – The Spice of (Night) Life. 49

Chapter 8: Around the Bedroom – Extra Dirty, Extra Naughty 56

Chapter 9: Holiday Humor – Naughty Under the Mistletoe and Beyond 62

Chapter 10: Holiday Humor – Naughty All Year Round 69

Chapter 11: Random and Outrageous – Anything Goes 76

Chapter 12: The Ultimate Naughty Collection – 100 Extra Spicy Jokes 88

Chapter 13: Make Your Friends Blush – Sharing Tips and Situational Humor 98

Chapter 14: Bonus Section – Extra Dirty Gems 105

Acknowledgments: To the Real Dirty Minds Behind the Laughs 112

Introduction: Buckle Up, Buttercup!

Welcome to "The Ultimate Collection of Dirty Jokes for Adults!"—a book that's here to make you laugh, cringe, and probably rethink a few life choices. Whether you stumbled upon this masterpiece intentionally or by sheer accident (sure, we'll believe that), one thing's for certain: you're in for a wild ride.

Now, let's get one thing straight: this book is not for everyone. If you're the kind of person who clutches their pearls at the mere mention of a *double entendre*, this might not be your cup of tea. In fact, you should probably put this book down immediately and go read something more wholesome—like a cookbook or an IKEA manual. But if you're the type who loves pushing boundaries and finds humor in the "did they really just say that?!" moments, then you've found your tribe.

We've packed this book with jokes so inappropriate, your grandma would faint if she even saw you holding it. (Unless your grandma's a legend. In that case, this one's for her.) You'll find everything from laugh-out-loud zingers to the kind of jokes that might get you banned from Thanksgiving dinner.

Before we dive in, here are a few friendly warnings:

1. This book will not make you a better person. In fact, it might make you worse. And honestly, isn't that the point?

2. You're probably going to laugh at something you shouldn't. It's okay. We won't tell. But, uh, maybe don't read this at work.

3. Some of these jokes are going to stick with you. Like that song you hate but can't stop humming. Only dirtier.

Oh, and one more thing: If you're here to judge, just remember—dirty minds think alike. Welcome to the club.

Now, grab a drink, settle in, and let's get to the good stuff. Fair warning: by the end of this book, you'll either be everyone's favorite comedian or banned from the group chat. Either way, it's gonna be worth it.

Let's get inappropriate, shall we?!

Chapter 1: Office Shenanigans

Ah, the workplace—a treasure trove of awkward moments, questionable behavior, and endless inspiration for inappropriate humor. Whether you're stuck in a cubicle or ruling from the corner office, we've all had those days when only a dirty joke can make the 9-to-5 grind bearable. Here are 50 hilarious, slightly inappropriate office jokes to keep you entertained (and probably on HR's radar).

1. Why don't office romances ever last?

Because they're all about *spread* sheets and not *bed* sheets.

2. My boss told me to think outside the box.

So, I went home early—there's no box there.

3. Why did the intern bring a ladder to work?

They heard the position had a lot of "climbing" opportunities.

4. What's an office worker's favorite type of party?

A *spreadsheet* party. Everyone gets laid... out in rows and columns.

5. Why did the stapler break up with the paper?

It couldn't handle the pressure of the attachment.

6. How do coworkers pass dirty notes?

On the *copier*. Extra copies for everyone.

7. What's the most NSFW thing in the office?

That one guy who still uses Internet Explorer.

8. Why did the accountant get fired?

They couldn't keep their assets covered.

9. What's the difference between my job and my love life?

At least my job comes with benefits.

10. Why don't pencils get involved in office drama?

They know it's all just *lead*ing to trouble.

11. My boss told me to "act professional."

So, I put on my best tie... and no pants.

12. Why was the copier so happy?

It finally got a toner date.

13. What do you call an office meeting with bad coffee?

A *brewhaha*.

14. How do office chairs flirt?

They offer to let you *take a spin*.

15. My coworker told me they were "working remotely."

Yeah, from the *bedroom*—with their partner.

16. Why did the printer break up with the scanner?

It was tired of being pushed *buttoned* all the time.

17. What's the sexiest thing about office supplies?

Rubber bands—they're so *flexible*.

18. My boss asked for a report on "team performance."

I sent them a list of bathroom break times.

19. Why don't office flings last long?

Because someone always *files* for separation.

20. What's the dirtiest thing in the breakroom?

The microwave. And *that one guy* who never cleans it.

21. Why are meetings like orgasms?

Half the time, they're fake.

22. Why did the HR manager blush?

They saw what happens on *Zoom* when you forget to turn off the camera.

23. Why are staplers bad at dating?

Because they're always looking for *clingy* types.

24. What's worse than office gossip?

That moment you realize you're the topic.

25. Why did the file cabinet get fired?

It couldn't keep its drawers shut.

26. What's the most inappropriate pickup line at work?

"Is that a presentation in your pocket, or are you just happy to see me?"

27. Why are office desks so moody?

They hate being *piled on.*

28. What did the sticky note say to the notebook?

"Let's stick together... but only for tonight."

29. Why don't office jokes go over well?

Because someone always takes them *personally*.

30. Why did the office supply manager get written up?

Caught with their pants down... by the *shredder*.

31. Why are employees like paper?

Because they're only useful until they're *crumpled*.

32. How does a workaholic spice up their love life?

By *merging cells* in the bedroom.

33. Why did the team leader get dumped?

They were way too *directive* in the relationship.

34. What's an office worker's favorite position?

Middle manager—no one expects much from you.

35. Why did the coffee machine file for harassment?

It was tired of being *poked* all the time.

36. What's the naughtiest office supply?

The white-out—it loves covering up *dirty mistakes.*

37. Why did the boss yell at the calendar?

Because it was full of *dates* they weren't invited to.

38. Why don't photocopiers ever lie?

Because they'll always give you *exact copies*.

39. Why are team-building exercises so awkward?

Because no one wants to *bond* outside of their browser tabs.

40. What's an office worker's worst fear?

That their *search history* gets printed out.

41. Why do computers hate office gossip?

They can't handle all the *uploads*.

42. What's the dirtiest thing about working from home?

The fact that no one wears pants.

43. Why did the office plant leave early?

It felt too *rooted* to one place.

44. Why did the manager refuse to date their assistant?

Because it would *Excel* their workload.

45. What's the most scandalous thing about a memo?

The way it gets *passed around* the office.

46. Why do office workers love pie charts?

Because they're always looking for a *slice* of something.

47. Why was the receptionist so popular?

Everyone wanted to be *on their calendar.*

48. Why do people love office happy hours?

Because it's the only time *bad decisions* are encouraged.

49. Why did the office printer call in sick?

It had a *paper jam* after an all-nighter.

50. What do you call a really attractive coworker?

A *HR violation* waiting to happen.

Chapter 2: Office Shenanigans – The After-Hours Edition!

Here's another batch of dirty jokes about the workplace, but this time, we're turning up the inappropriateness to *NSFW* levels. These jokes might just get you escorted out by HR—if you dare to share them at work!

1. Why did the stapler get arrested?

For pinning someone down without consent.

2. What do you call a photocopier that gets around?

A *serial reproducer.*

3. Why don't office chairs date coworkers?

Because they're tired of being *sat on.*

4. Why did the office printer break up with the scanner?

Because it found someone with better curves.

5. What's the dirtiest thing in the office?

That one corner where the janitor doesn't *clean up properly.*

6. Why did the intern blush?

Because they caught the boss *handling his paperwork* a little too enthusiastically.

7. Why don't staplers make good lovers?

Because they always *get stuck* halfway.

8. What's worse than being micromanaged?

When your boss wants to *get hands-on.*

9. Why did the office plant get moved to the breakroom?

It kept watching *too much action* at night.

10. Why did the IT guy bring a condom to work?

Because someone told him to *protect his hard drive.*

11. What's the best part about working late?

No one's around to see you *play with your tools.*

12. Why do office desks love drama?

Because they're always getting *on top of things.*

13. Why did the coworker's shirt look wrinkled?

Because they spent the night *crumpling someone else's papers.*

14. What's the worst thing you can say in a meeting?

"*Does this presentation make you as hot as it makes me?*"

15. Why don't coffee machines date printers?

Because they're afraid of *steaming things up.*

16. My boss said I need to learn how to "manage upward."

I told them I'm already great at *climbing the ladder.*

17. Why did the office cleaner quit?

Because they were tired of wiping up *messy deposits.*

18. Why did the HR manager blush?

They walked in on the copier *handling someone's assets.*

19. Why did the IT department start locking doors?

Because people kept trying to *turn them on.*

20. What's the dirtiest thing in the breakroom?

The microwave. And the *coworkers who keep heating up trouble.*

21. Why don't coworkers share bedsheets?

Because they don't want to *spread out the workload.*

22. What's the fastest way to spice up an office party?

Whisper, "Who wants to see my *PowerPoint presentation* in private?"

23. Why did the office keyboard go to therapy?

It was tired of being *pressed all day long.*

24. Why do office supplies hate romantic relationships?

Because someone always ends up *getting stapled down.*

25. What's worse than being underpaid?

Being *under someone who can't perform.*

26. Why do printers make terrible partners?

Because they love to *jam up the action.*

27. Why did the office door lock itself?

It didn't want to hear about another coworker's *open-door policy.*

28. What's an IT guy's favorite type of foreplay?

Plugging it in and turning it on.

29. Why don't pencils ever get laid?

Because they're always too *sharpened to connect.*

30. What do you call a team-building retreat gone wrong?

An *all-inclusive orgy of bad decisions.*

31. Why did the copier file a complaint?

It was tired of people *exposing themselves* on it.

32. Why do staplers make bad lovers?

Because they're all about *quick finishes.*

33. What's the dirtiest thing you can do at work?

Open someone's *search history.*

34. Why did the boss install cameras in the breakroom?

Because someone kept *making steamy scenes.*

35. Why don't meetings ever lead to satisfaction?

Because no one knows how to *wrap things up properly.*

36. Why did the receptionist wear sunglasses?

Because everyone was too *bright and exposed* that day.

37. What's the kinkiest thing about the office?

The way *cubicles encourage secret rendezvous.*

38. Why did the intern quit after a week?

Because they were tired of being asked to *bend over backwards.*

39. What's worse than Monday mornings?

A *coworker who thinks they're your boss in bed.*

40. Why did the office fridge get fired?

Because it couldn't stop *freezing people out.*

41. Why don't paper clips hook up?

Because they're afraid of *getting twisted in knots.*

42. What's the most scandalous thing to do at work?

Printing personal documents on company time.

43. Why did the boss install tinted windows?

To *block out all the inappropriate views.*

44. What's the dirtiest file in the office?

The one marked *"secret projects"* that everyone knows about.

45. Why do coworkers love coffee breaks?

Because it's the only time they can *spill without consequences.*

46. What do you call a sexy office chair?

One that loves to *recline in all the right places.*

47. Why did the boss ban casual Fridays?

Too many employees started showing up *half-dressed.*

48. What's the best way to kill productivity?

Whisper, "Want to see my *hard drive*?"

49. Why don't office romances last?

Because someone always gets *paper-shredded in the process.*

50. What's worse than being underpaid?

Realizing you're also *undervalued in bed.*

These jokes are definitely not safe for work, but they'll leave you crying with laughter if shared with the right crowd!

Chapter 3: Relationships – Love, Lust, and Everything In Between

Ah, relationships. The only thing messier than an office desk on a Monday morning. From romantic misadventures to steamy encounters, this chapter dives into the hilariously inappropriate side of love, dating, and marriage. Get ready to laugh, blush, and maybe even send a few of these to your partner (if they can handle it).

1. Why did the couple bring a ladder to the bedroom?

They heard it could help them *reach new heights*.

2. My partner told me I'm bad at pillow talk.

So now I just talk about *feathers* and *thread counts*.

3. What do you call a couple who only fights in bed?

Pillow *fighters*.

4. Why did the newlyweds get kicked out of the restaurant?

They couldn't keep their hands off each other's *breadsticks*.

5. Why do married couples love puzzles?

Because putting the pieces together is the only action they're getting.

6. My partner asked me what I wanted for dinner.

I said, "You... on a platter." They laughed. I didn't.

7. Why did the ex start a bakery?

Because they were so good at making people *crumble*.

8. What's a hopeless romantic's favorite position?

On one knee... begging.

9. Why don't love triangles ever work out?

Because someone always gets *cornered*.

10. Why did the vibrator break up with the battery?

It couldn't handle the lack of *energy*.

11. My partner told me to spice things up in the bedroom.

So, I brought cayenne pepper. They were not impressed.

12. Why don't relationships in gyms last?

Because everyone's just *working out* their options.

13. My girlfriend asked if she looked fat in her dress.

I told her she looked like a *snack*. Now I'm single.

14. Why do single people always sleep better?

Because they don't have someone *stealing the covers*... or their will to live.

15. What's the difference between love and a good steak?

One's rare. The other's medium-rare.

16. Why did the breakup feel like a game of hide-and-seek?

Because someone just didn't want to be *found*.

17. My partner told me to act like an adult in bed.

So, I filled out taxes while crying.

18. Why don't couples play Monopoly anymore?

Because someone always ends up *bankrupting* their relationship.

19. What's the fastest way to ruin a date?

Mention your *exes*. Bonus points if you do it in alphabetical order.

20. Why don't ghosts go on dates?

They don't have the *spirit* for commitment.

21. My partner said we should role-play.

So, I pretended I didn't hear them.

22. What's a wedding DJ's favorite pickup line?

"Let me *spin* you right round."

23. Why did the wife throw her husband out of bed?

She was tired of his *snoring*… and his jokes.

24. What's the most romantic thing you can say during a fight?

"Baby, you're right. I'm wrong. Let's get *naked*."

25. Why are relationships like Wi-Fi signals?

They start strong, then drop when you're in the other room.

26. What's the difference between dating and marriage?

Dating is like streaming—exciting and new. Marriage is *buffering*… forever.

27. Why did the bachelor get cold feet?

He realized he couldn't just *Ctrl+Z* the wedding.

28. What do you call a partner who loves texting but hates talking?

A *phoney* lover.

29. Why do couples fight during vacations?

Because love can't fix a *terrible itinerary*.

30. My partner asked why I don't write them poetry.

So, I wrote: "Roses are red, violets are blue, I like pizza more than I like you."

31. Why did the husband install a mirror on the ceiling?

To reflect on their *love life*.

32. Why did the boyfriend buy a telescope?

Because he wanted to *look deeper* into their relationship.

33. Why don't relationships work with bad texters?

Because you'll always be left *on read*.

34. Why did the couple bring dice to bed?

Because they wanted to *roll with it*.

35. What's a hopeless romantic's biggest fear?

Getting ghosted... by a *real ghost*.

36. Why did Cupid get fired from his job?

Too many *premature shots*.

37. What's a married man's least favorite word?

"*Honey-do* list."

38. Why are long-distance relationships so hard?

Because you can't send *physical emojis*.

39. Why did the wife lock the door?

She wanted a night of *peace and quiet*... without her husband.

40. Why do men hate shopping with their partners?

Because "five more minutes" actually means *forever*.

41. What's the difference between a relationship and a phone charger?

At least the charger *knows how to connect*.

42. Why did the couple argue during karaoke?

Because one of them hit the wrong *notes*... in life.

43. Why don't people in love ever sleep?

Because they're busy *dreaming* of each other... or watching Netflix.

44. Why did the couple take separate vacations?

To find themselves—and then lose each other.

45. Why do some men refuse to ask for directions?

Because they already lost their way *in the relationship.*

46. What's a single person's favorite holiday?

Black Friday. No one to tell you *how much to spend.*

47. Why are anniversaries like taxes?

Because if you forget, you'll *pay for it.*

48. Why did the partner cancel date night?

Too much *Netflix cheating*.

49. What's a hopeless romantic's favorite song?

"*All By Myself*"... on repeat.

50. Why did the boyfriend take his girlfriend to a buffet?

Because he wanted to see how much she could *handle*.

Chapter 4: Relationships – Love, Lust, and Everything In Between (Extra Dirty Edition)

Let's dive headfirst into the hilariously dirty and downright inappropriate side of love, dating, and everything that happens (or doesn't happen) behind closed doors. These jokes aren't just risqué—they're the kind you probably shouldn't tell on a first date... unless your date is as wild as you are.

1. Why don't relationships ever work in bed?

Because someone always gets *off* too early.

2. My partner told me I was like a vibrator.

Reliable but lacking *emotion.*

3. Why don't men ever ask for directions?

Because they don't even know how to find the *right spot.*

4. What do you call it when two people kiss and accidentally bite?

A *love nibble,* or so they claim.

5. Why don't love triangles ever work?

Because someone always ends up *pointed in the wrong direction.*

6. My girlfriend told me to "make her scream."

So, I showed her my *credit card statement.*

7. Why did the couple fight in the hot tub?

Because one of them kept *blowing bubbles.*

8. Why don't relationships in gyms work?

Because everyone's too busy *flexing for attention.*

9. My partner told me they love it when I get dirty.

So, I didn't shower for a week. Now I'm single.

10. Why do married couples never play hide and seek?

Because no one wants to *be found naked.*

11. What's the worst thing to hear in bed?

"Is it in yet?"

12. Why did the couple bring dice to bed?

They wanted to *roll the odds of getting lucky.*

13. What's the kinkiest thing about relationships?

The way you keep coming back even after being *tied down.*

14. Why don't relationships last past three months?

Because that's when the *filters come off.*

15. What's worse than a bad date?

One that ends with "*Can I borrow $20?*"

16. Why do couples love hotel rooms?

Because no one can hear you *complain about their snoring.*

17. Why did the vibrator break up with its owner?

It felt *overused and underappreciated.*

18. What's a romantic's favorite part of the body?

The *heart*. But we all know they're lying.

19. Why did the honeymoon end early?

Too much *role-playing* and not enough sleep.

20. Why don't people propose in bed?

Because they're too busy trying to *finish first.*

21. What's worse than being ghosted?

Finding out your ghoster is now *haunting your best friend.*

22. My partner told me to spice things up.

So, I brought chili powder to bed. That was a *hot mess.*

23. Why don't couples ever argue during sex?

Because they're *too busy faking it.*

24. What's the difference between love and lust?

About three hours and a bottle of tequila.

25. Why do people fall for bad texters?

Because they're *masters of leaving you unsatisfied.*

26. What's a hopeless romantic's worst fear?

Realizing their partner only loves them for their *Netflix password.*

27. Why did the girlfriend break up with the dentist?

She was tired of all the *drilling with no climax.*

28. Why don't relationships last through the holidays?

Because someone always *unwraps the wrong package.*

29. Why did the couple stop kissing?

Because one of them whispered, "*I just farted.*"

30. Why do candles make the best lovers?

Because they know how to *melt you in all the right places.*

31. Why did the wife get kicked out of the yoga class?

For *downward-dogging* the instructor.

32. Why don't people hook up in the rain?

Because it's too hard to tell the difference between *wet and wetter.*

33. What's worse than a bad kiss?

One that comes with *accidental teeth grinding.*

34. Why did the girlfriend slap her boyfriend?

Because he asked if she *wanted to watch porn together.* (She said yes later.)

35. Why don't exes ever stay friends?

Because they're still *trying to win the breakup.*

36. Why did the husband sleep on the couch?

Because the wife told him to *keep his hands to himself.*

37. Why do newlyweds smile so much?

Because they haven't *unpacked the baggage* yet.

38. What's the worst kind of rejection?

When they say, "*Let's just be friends.*" No thanks.

39. Why don't long-distance relationships work?

Because no one can handle *phone sex buffering.*

40. Why are pickup lines so terrible?

Because the good ones are only used by *people who don't need them.*

41. Why did the bed frame complain?

Because it couldn't handle all the *banging.*

42. What's a hopeless romantic's favorite activity?

Dreaming about someone who doesn't even know they exist.

43. Why don't people send love letters anymore?

Because *nudes get the point across faster.*

44. Why did the girlfriend throw her boyfriend's phone?

Because she saw his *Tinder matches.*

45. What's a couple's favorite holiday?

Valentine's Day—for the *excuse to try new positions.*

46. Why don't roses make good apologies?

Because they *prick more than they please.*

47. What's worse than cheating?

Getting caught and having to *explain why your phone was unlocked.*

48. Why do married people love vacation sex?

Because it's the only time they can *pretend they're single.*

49. Why don't people flirt in the grocery store?

Because *bananas are too obvious.*

50. What's the worst thing to hear during a breakup?

"I never loved you; I just really loved your dog."

Did you laugh, groan, or blush? Shall we move on to Bar Banter or keep diving into relationships?

Chapter 5: Bar Banter – Drinks, Laughs, and Inappropriate Shenanigans

There's something about a dimly lit bar, a cold drink, and bad decisions that makes dirty jokes flow like tequila at happy hour. Whether you're sipping, slamming, or slurring, this chapter is packed with the kind of humor that'll get you free drinks… or kicked out entirely.

1. Why don't bartenders ever date their customers?

Because they've seen them after *five shots*.

2. What do you call a tequila shot with a lime wedge?

A bad decision waiting to happen.

3. My date said, "You're like a fine wine."

Turns out they meant I'm better after they've had a few glasses.

4. Why don't cocktails have kids?

Because they can't find the right *mixer*.

5. What's a bartender's favorite type of foreplay?

Shaking things up before it gets *stirred*.

6. Why did the beer get rejected at the bar?

It was too *flat* to be attractive.

7. Why are margaritas like your ex?

They're sweet, salty, and leave you with a headache in the morning.

8. What did the whiskey glass say to the vodka bottle?

"You're *basic,* but I'll still take a shot."

9. Why did the bar stool get jealous?

Because the bartender kept giving everyone else a *lap dance*.

10. What's the difference between a good bartender and a bad lover?

One knows how to handle a *stiff pour.*

11. Why did the drunk girl bring a pillow to the bar?

She heard it was the perfect place to *pick someone up*.

12. What's a martini's favorite type of foreplay?

Getting a good *shake* before the action starts.

13. Why did the beer bottle break up with the shot glass?

Because it was tired of being a *one-night stand*.

14. Why are bartenders the best in bed?

Because they know how to *mix things up*.

15. What's the bartender's least favorite customer?

The one who starts with, "What's the strongest thing you've got?" and ends with, "Can I get a water?"

16. Why did the mojito flirt with the rum punch?

Because it couldn't resist that *minty freshness.*

17. What's a tequila's favorite pickup line?

"Let's get salty and lick things off each other."

18. Why did the vodka tonic start crying?

It heard someone say it's a "basic bitch" drink.

19. What's a wine bottle's idea of foreplay?

A little twist, a pop, and some gentle pouring.

20. Why did the beer leave the party early?

It couldn't handle all the *foam play*.

21. Why did the drunk guy flirt with the bartender?

Because he wanted to see if they could *handle his tip*.

22. What's a hangover's best pickup line?

"Remember me? I made last night unforgettable… and this morning unbearable."

23. Why don't whiskey drinkers trust gin lovers?

Because they're always *mixing things up*.

24. Why did the cocktail apologize?

Because it couldn't handle the *hard liquor*.

25. What do you call a flirtatious glass of wine?

A *Cabernet Can't-Say-No*.

26. Why did the drunk girl take her beer to the dance floor?

She wanted to see if it could *tap that*.

27. Why are bartenders so good in relationships?

Because they know when to *pour more* and when to *cut you off*.

28. What's the difference between a bartender and a stripper?

One makes you tipsy, the other makes you *tip*.

29. Why don't drunk people ever remember their nights out?

Because tequila erases *more than just boundaries*.

30. Why did the gin and tonic stop dating?

Because it wasn't a *tonic* relationship.

31. What's the dirtiest thing about a bar?

That one corner where drunk couples *think no one's watching*.

32. Why did the whiskey want a threesome?

Because it loves being *on the rocks*.

33. What's the worst thing you can hear at a bar?

"We're out of alcohol, but we've got plenty of water."

34. Why are margaritas always the life of the party?

Because they're salty, sweet, and know how to *rim things just right*.

35. What do you call a drunk guy hitting on everyone?

An *equal opportunity offender*.

36. Why did the bartender quit?

They got tired of people asking, "Is this drink *strong enough*?"

37. What's a drunk girl's favorite song?

"Pour Some Sugar on Me"... literally.

38. Why don't wine drinkers ever commit?

Because they love to keep their *options corked*.

39. Why did the beer keg refuse to go to the party?

Because it didn't want to get *tapped* again.

40. What's a vodka bottle's least favorite customer?

The one who orders a "vodka soda" and *pretends they're fancy*.

41. Why did the drunk guy take his shirt off?

Because the tequila told him he was a *model*.

42. What do you call a drunk girl who's lost her friends?

A *wanderlust queen*... with no direction.

43. Why did the cocktail glass blush?

Because it got *dirty shaken*.

44. Why are bars the best place for hookups?

Because everyone's already *lowered their standards*.

45. Why don't bartenders date customers?

Because they're tired of *mixed signals.*

46. What's a bar fight's best weapon?

The *truth* after four shots of whiskey.

47. Why do tequila drinkers always make the worst decisions?

Because they leave their *common sense* in the salt rim.

48. Why did the gin bottle cry?

Because it saw someone order a *vodka martini*.

49. What's the bartender's favorite way to flirt?

By asking, "Want me to make you something *hard*?"

50. Why did the shot glass refuse to party?

Because it couldn't handle *all the tipsy drama.*

Shall we shake up another chapter or keep the drinks flowing?

Chapter 6: Bar Banter – Where the Drinks Flow and Standards Lower

Bars are where bad decisions are made, flirty remarks fly, and dirty jokes get funnier with every drink. These extra dirty bar jokes will have you laughing (or cringing) as you imagine just how many of these might have actually happened after a few shots.

1. Why did the tequila get dumped?

Because it left everyone with *trust issues and bad decisions.*

2. Why don't bartenders ever date customers?

Because they've seen them *hit rock bottom—and then hit on a potted plant.*

3. What's a drunk person's favorite type of romance?

One-night *stirred*.

4. Why did the martini glass blush?

Because someone kept asking it to *get dirty*.

5. Why are bar stools such flirts?

Because they're always *ready to support your ass*.

6. What do you call a cocktail that never satisfies?

A *whiskey tease*.

7. Why did the drunk guy keep rubbing his beer?

Because he thought it was a *genie bottle*.

8. What's a bartender's favorite game?

"*Let's see who tips better.*"

9. Why don't vodka bottles ever hook up?

Because they're too *stiff to make the first move*.

10. Why do rum drinkers make the worst partners?

Because they're always *pirating someone else's booty*.

11. What's the sexiest thing about a mojito?

The way it gets you *minty fresh for bad decisions.*

12. Why don't shot glasses ever date each other?

Because they're *all about quick finishes.*

13. What's the dirtiest thing you can say at a bar?

"*Want to see how well I handle a long neck?*"

14. Why did the whiskey cry at the bar?

Because it couldn't handle all the *blended emotions.*

15. Why do bars love karaoke?

Because it's the only time drunk people get to *hit high notes.*

16. What's the worst pickup line at a bar?

"*You look like someone who'd appreciate a free drink... and bad company.*"

17. Why did the wine glass flirt with the champagne flute?

Because it wanted to know how it *stayed so bubbly.*

18. What's a cocktail's favorite kind of foreplay?

Getting *shaken and stirred* in all the right places.

19. Why did the margarita break up with the salt shaker?

Because it got tired of all the *rimming*.

20. Why don't beer drinkers ever commit?

Because they're always chasing their *next round*.

21. Why do drunk people make terrible lovers?

Because they're always *spilling everything*.

22. What's a bartender's least favorite phrase?

"*Make me something strong but fruity.*"

23. Why did the vodka tonic start a fight?

Because someone called it *basic*.

24. What's the best drink for a bad date?

Something that's *strong enough to forget their name*.

25. Why do people love wine tastings?

Because they can get *classy drunk* and still flirt with strangers.

26. What's the sexiest thing about a margarita?

The way it makes you forget your *standards*.

27. Why did the beer keg refuse to leave the bar?

Because it didn't want to get *tapped out*.

28. Why do rum punches make the best lovers?

Because they know how to *mix it up*.

29. What's a drunk's favorite kind of dance?

The *floor spin.*

30. Why did the bartender call in sick?

Because they couldn't handle any more *bad pickup lines.*

31. Why don't wine bottles make good wingmen?

Because they're *always getting cork-blocked.*

32. What's the worst thing to hear at a bar?

"We've run out of *alcohol."*

33. Why did the cocktail glass refuse a second date?

Because it didn't like being *manhandled.*

34. Why do bars make the best places for hookups?

Because everyone's *lowered their standards by drink three.*

35. What's the sexiest thing about a bar fight?

The *makeup drinking* afterward.

36. Why did the drunk guy keep looking at the ceiling?

Because someone told him he was *raising the bar.*

37. What's the difference between a martini and a date?

A martini always leaves you *feeling better afterward.*

38. Why do bartenders love late nights?

Because it's when the *tips and shirts come off.*

39. Why don't people flirt with their bartender?

Because they know they'll *never measure up.*

40. Why did the beer bottle blush?

Because it saw someone *deep-throat a straw.*

41. What's the difference between a hangover and a bad ex?

At least the hangover is *gone by noon.*

42. Why do wine drinkers make the best lovers?

Because they know how to *linger and savor.*

43. What's the worst thing to hear at last call?

"*That's it?*"

44. Why did the bartender refuse to serve the naked guy?

Because he didn't have the right *tips.*

45. Why don't rum bottles ever lie?

Because they're *transparent about getting you into trouble.*

46. What's the dirtiest thing you can say to a bartender?

"Give me something wet and slippery."

47. Why did the gin and tonic start dating?

Because they're both *tonic-ally attracted.*

48. Why do shots make the best wingmen?

Because they'll have you *hooking up in no time.*

49. What's worse than a spilled drink?

The *sob story* that comes after it.

50. Why do bartenders have the best stories?

Because they've seen *more action in one night* than most people do in a year.

These jokes are as wild as a Friday night happy hour. Ready to spice things up with Around the Bedroom jokes? Let's get even dirtier!

Chapter 7: Around the Bedroom – The Spice of (Night) Life

The bedroom is where the magic happens—or at least where it's supposed to happen. Whether it's a wild night or a total disaster, this chapter is dedicated to jokes that'll make you laugh so hard, you might need to change the sheets (again). Let's dive under the covers for some humor that's as spicy as your *search history*.

1. Why did the bed break?

It couldn't handle all the *horizontal hustle.*

2. My partner said I should whisper something dirty in their ear.

So, I said, *"The dishes are still in the sink."*

3. Why don't people tell secrets in bed?

Because they always end up *spread out.*

4. What's a blanket's favorite move in bed?

The *wrap-around-and-snuggle.*

5. Why did the pillow fight get so intense?

Because someone wanted to *get stuffed.*

6. Why don't condoms ever tell lies?

Because they're *transparent* about protection.

7. My girlfriend asked me to turn her on.

So I flipped the *light switch...* and then she flipped me off.

8. What do you call a mattress that's seen too much action?

Over-sprung and under-appreciated.

9. Why did the vibrator go on strike?

Because it was tired of doing all the *hard work*.

10. My partner said we should try role-playing in bed.

So I pretended I had *energy* after 9 p.m.

11. Why are bedrooms so noisy?

Because the walls can't handle all the *bed squeaks and giggles.*

12. What's the worst thing to hear during a romantic moment?

"Did you take the trash out?"

13. Why did the couple argue about the blanket?

Because someone always ends up *bare-assed and cold.*

14. What's the kinkiest piece of furniture?

The *headboard.* It's always banging.

15. My partner asked me to spice things up.

So I brought in chili powder. They weren't impressed.

16. Why do some people hate hotel beds?

Because they don't come with the *sounds of home.*

17. What's a one-night stand's worst nightmare?

Getting stuck in someone's *family group chat.*

18. Why do light switches love romance?

Because they're always *on and off.*

19. What's a couple's favorite song in bed?

"Let's Get It *On.*"

20. Why did the mirror blush?

Because it saw *everything.*

21. What's the sexiest kind of music?

Sheets-metal.

22. My partner said they wanted "breakfast in bed."

So I threw them a Pop-Tart and went back to sleep.

23. Why are curtains the ultimate wingmen?

Because they'll always *cover for you.*

24. Why don't blankets ever cheat?

Because they're all about *keeping you warm.*

25. Why are beds so great at keeping secrets?

Because they're masters of *pillow talk.*

26. What's the difference between a bed and a lover?

A bed will always *support* you.

27. My partner said we should try something new in bed.

So I brought *snacks.*

28. Why did the sexy pillow get dumped?

Because it was too *soft* for the job.

29. Why are duvets like bad lovers?

Because they're *impossible to manage.*

30. What's a partner's least favorite phrase in bed?

"Wait, what's that noise?"

31. Why don't couples ever nap after sex?

Because they're too busy *recovering.*

32. Why is the floor jealous of the bed?

Because it never gets to *feel the love.*

33. What's the biggest bedroom turn-off?

Cold feet—and not the metaphorical kind.

34. Why are sheets so dependable?

Because they'll always *cover your ass.*

35. What's a couple's favorite board game in bed?

Twister.

36. Why don't people invite their pets into the bedroom?

Because they don't need an audience for their *awkward moves.*

37. What's the dirtiest thing in the bedroom?

That *unwashed sock* under the bed.

38. Why do some people hate memory foam?

Because it remembers *everything.*

39. My partner said they wanted more action in bed.

So I started doing *karate.*

40. Why are bedrooms so underrated?

Because they're the stage for the best *performances.*

41. Why do couples love pillows so much?

Because they're the ultimate *comfort zones.*

42. What's the biggest bedroom mistake?

Using *too much lube.* Trust me.

43. Why don't beds like threesomes?

Because someone always ends up on the *floor.*

44. Why did the lamp feel left out?

Because it wasn't part of the *action.*

45. What's the most awkward part of morning sex?

Realizing you forgot to *brush your teeth.*

46. Why don't couples use waterbeds anymore?

Because they're tired of *drowning in regret.*

47. Why is the bedroom the best room in the house?

Because it's where you can be *completely yourself.*

48. What's the dirtiest secret in the bedroom?

That *unfolded laundry pile* in the corner.

49. Why don't partners ever agree on pillows?

Because everyone has their own *comfort zones.*

50. What's the best way to keep things exciting in bed?

Never let your partner *fall asleep first.*

That's enough to keep you *tossing and turning*! Ready for the next chapter, or want to explore a different vibe?

Chapter 8: Around the Bedroom – Extra Dirty, Extra Naughty

The bedroom is where fantasies come alive— or at least where you realize your partner left the laundry on the bed again. These extra dirty bedroom jokes will make you laugh, blush, and maybe even give you some ideas for later.

1. Why did the bed file for divorce?

Because it was tired of being *banged around* with no appreciation.

2. My partner told me to spice things up in bed.

So, I brought a bottle of sriracha. It was a *hot mess.*

3. What's worse than bad sex?

When they say, "*Did you finish?*" and you didn't even *start*.

4. Why don't beds ever cheat?

Because they're too busy *supporting everyone's baggage*.

5. What's a blanket's favorite move in bed?

The *wrap-around-and-tuck*.

6. Why did the pillow break up with the mattress?

Because it couldn't handle all the *pressure* anymore.

7. Why don't mirrors make good lovers?

Because they're *too focused on themselves.*

8. What's the dirtiest thing you can do in bed?

Forget to wash the sheets after a *wild night.*

9. Why don't vibrators ever ghost you?

Because they're always *charged and ready.*

10. My partner asked for a threesome.

So, I brought in *Netflix and snacks.*

11. Why did the mattress feel dirty?

Because it saw *too much action* in one night.

12. What's worse than a bad kisser?

One who leaves your face feeling like a *slip-and-slide.*

13. Why don't nightstands flirt?

Because they're tired of being *used and ignored.*

14. What's the most awkward thing to hear in bed?

"Oh… I thought you knew how to do that."

15. Why do couples fight in the bedroom?

Because someone always *steals the blanket.*

16. Why did the headboard call the cops?

Because it couldn't handle all the *banging.*

17. What's a bed's favorite workout?

Jumping jacks, but only if you're doing it right.

18. Why don't condoms tell jokes?

Because they don't want to be *stretched too thin.*

19. Why did the sheets blush?

Because they saw what the pillows were *up to.*

20. What's worse than being bad in bed?

When they say, "*You're cute when you try.*"

21. Why did the vibrator go on strike?

Because it felt *overworked and underpaid.*

22. Why don't couples use waterbeds anymore?

Because no one wants to *drown in regret.*

23. What's a lamp's favorite bedroom activity?

Turning on and staying that way.

24. Why don't beds ever judge?

Because they've *seen it all.*

25. What's the worst thing to bring to bed?

A *grudge—and maybe cold feet.*

26. Why don't blankets ever date?

Because they can't handle *too much heat.*

27. What's a mattress's biggest fear?

Getting sprung too soon.

28. Why did the pillow start therapy?

Because it couldn't handle being *smothered every night.*

29. What's the best way to ruin the mood in bed?

Answering a work email.

30. Why did the bedroom window laugh?

Because it saw *everything you were trying to hide.*

31. Why don't candles ever cheat?

Because they're *burning for just one.*

32. What's the dirtiest thing you can whisper in bed?

"I forgot to take the trash out."

33. Why don't fans ever join the action?

Because they're too busy *blowing everything else.*

34. Why did the mattress file a complaint?

Because someone kept *rolling around without permission.*

35. What's the best kind of bedroom talk?

The kind that ends with *laughter and a little sweat.*

36. Why don't mirrors get invited to threesomes?

Because they're already *seeing double.*

37. What's worse than a boring partner in bed?

Someone who *talks about their ex.*

38. Why did the bed refuse to move?

Because it was *tired of carrying the load.*

39. What's a lamp's worst nightmare?

Getting *turned off* right before the good part.

40. Why don't couples use pillows during fights?

Because they don't want to *mess up the fluff.*

41. Why did the couple take dice to bed?

To see how many *positions they could roll for.*

42. Why don't curtains ever date?

Because they're *always drawn to the wrong types.*

43. What's worse than bad sex?

Hearing "*Let's just cuddle instead.*"

44. Why don't duvets ever flirt?

Because they're too busy *covering up mistakes.*

45. What's the dirtiest thing in the bedroom?

That *unwashed sock* under the bed.

46. Why do couples love hotel sex?

Because *no one has to do the laundry afterward.*

47. Why don't carpets ever join the fun?

Because they're *always getting walked on.*

48. What's the dirtiest secret in bed?

All the crumbs from *midnight snacks.*

49. Why did the pillow refuse to cuddle?

Because it felt *too fluffed up already.*

50. What's the kinkiest thing about blankets?

They know how to *wrap things up just right.*

The bedroom just got a whole lot steamier—and funnier! Shall we keep rolling with Holiday Humor or take things in another direction?

Chapter 9: Holiday Humor – Naughty Under the Mistletoe and Beyond

Ah, the holidays—a time for family, food, and highly questionable decisions fueled by eggnog, mulled wine, and the lingering awkwardness of having your drunk uncle around. This chapter brings you the funniest and naughtiest holiday-themed jokes that'll make you the star of the party... or get you permanently uninvited.

1. Why did Santa's elf get fired?

He kept making *inappropriate stocking stuffers.*

2. What's Santa's favorite position?

On top of his *naughty list.*

3. Why did the turkey refuse to play in the band?

Because it didn't want to get *stuffed*… again.

4. What's the difference between a snowman and a snowwoman?

Snowballs.

5. Why do ghosts make terrible lovers?

Because they just don't have the *spirit* for it.

6. What's the sexiest thing about Halloween?

The *tricks* are just as good as the *treats.*

7. Why did the Easter Bunny skip foreplay?

Because it was all about *quick hops.*

8. What's Santa's worst nightmare?

Accidentally walking in on Mrs. Claus *polishing the sleigh* with the elves.

9. Why don't skeletons have girlfriends?

Because they don't have the *guts* to ask anyone out.

10. Why is mistletoe so scandalous?

Because it gets people *tongue-tied.*

11. What do you call a reindeer who likes to party?

Dasher—for obvious reasons.

12. Why did Cupid get grounded?

Too many *premature arrows.*

13. What's the difference between Thanksgiving dinner and great sex?

You'll probably want seconds of *only one* of them.

14. Why did the Valentine's Day card blush?

Because it saw the envelope *getting licked.*

15. Why are New Year's resolutions like one-night stands?

They both seem like a good idea at midnight... and a terrible one the next morning.

16. What's the Easter Bunny's favorite pickup line?

"Do you want to see my *carrot*?"

17. Why is Christmas dinner like a bad date?

You spend hours prepping, and someone always leaves *unsatisfied.*

18. Why do witches love Halloween?

Because they get to *ride all night.*

19. What's the dirtiest holiday?

April Fools' Day—because nothing is *as it seems.*

20. Why did the gingerbread man get arrested?

Indecent exposure of his *icing*.

21. Why don't reindeer ever get married?

Because they hate being *tied down*.

22. What's the naughtiest Christmas decoration?

The *wreath*—it's always *going in circles*.

23. Why did Santa cancel his date with the tooth fairy?

Because he didn't want to end up *biting off more than he could chew*.

24. What's Cupid's favorite kind of kiss?

The kind that involves *tongue and a few regrets*.

25. Why don't Christmas lights ever hook up?

Because they always get *tangled*.

26. Why did the pumpkin break up with its partner?

Because it felt *hollow inside*.

27. What's the best way to spice up Valentine's Day?

Forget flowers—bring *chocolate and handcuffs*.

28. Why don't turkeys ever get laid?

Because they're always too *stuffed* to move.

29. Why do drunk Santas make the worst dates?

Because they'll come down your *chimney* but never call you back.

30. What's the raciest thing about Easter?

All those *hidden eggs*.

31. Why are Halloween costumes so sexy these days?

Because everyone's trying to show off their *booty*.

32. What's Santa's favorite game?

Hide the *candy cane.*

33. Why did the snowman flirt with the sun?

Because it wanted to feel *hot* for once.

34. What's the difference between Christmas morning and a great date?

You only unwrap one of them with *anticipation.*

35. Why did the sleigh ride turn romantic?

Because Santa always knows how to *slide in smoothly.*

36. What's the sexiest Christmas song?

"All I Want for Christmas is *You*"—especially after a few drinks.

37. Why don't elves date each other?

Because they're tired of *small talk.*

38. What's the dirtiest thing you can say on Thanksgiving?

"Pass the gravy, baby."

39. Why did the Easter Bunny fail at online dating?

Too many *bad eggs* in the basket.

40. What's Santa's favorite pickup line?

"Want to see if my sleigh *rides well*?"

41. Why don't Christmas stockings hook up?

Because they always get *hung up.*

42. What do ghosts say during foreplay?

"*Boo-me.*"

43. Why do turkeys make bad lovers?

Because they finish way too *fast.*

44. What's a reindeer's favorite move?

The *sleigh and stay.*

45. Why did the snowman flirt with the snowwoman?

Because she looked *frosty fine.*

46. What's a skeleton's favorite position?

Bone-to-bone.

47. Why did the mistletoe break up with the holly?

Because it wanted to *branch out.*

48. What's the sexiest thing about fireworks?

The *explosions* at the end.

49. Why do Christmas trees love ornaments?

Because they love getting *decked out*.

50. Why don't elves ever relax?

Because they're always *wrapping things up.*

The holidays will never feel the same! Are we moving on to Random and Outrageous or cooking up another chapter?

Chapter 10: Holiday Humor – Naughty All Year Round

Holidays are a time for family, food, and festivities... but let's not forget the dirty jokes that make the celebrations even more fun. These extra inappropriate holiday jokes will have you laughing so hard, you might spill the eggnog.

Christmas Dirty Jokes

1. Why did Santa get a divorce? Because Mrs. Claus found his *sack in someone else's chimney.*

2. What's the dirtiest Christmas song? "All I Want for Christmas is *You*... and maybe your friend, too."

3. Why did the reindeer blush? Because it saw Santa *polishing his candy cane.*

4. What's the naughtiest thing you can say at a Christmas party? "Who wants to sit on my *lap and make a wish?"*

5. Why don't elves date each other? Because they're tired of *shortcomings.*

6. What did Mrs. Claus say when Santa came home early? *"Did you finish delivering already?"*

7. Why did the Christmas tree refuse to go home with the drunk guy? Because it didn't want to get *lit again.*

8. What's Santa's favorite pickup line? "Let me slide down your *chimney tonight."*

9. Why do Christmas lights love the holidays? Because they get to *turn everyone on.*

10. What's Santa's worst nightmare? Walking in on Mrs. Claus *stuffing someone else's stockings.*

Halloween Dirty Jokes

11. Why don't skeletons ever have sex? Because they don't have the *guts.*

12. What's a witch's favorite position? *On her broomstick*—but only at full moon.

13. Why did the vampire get dumped? Because he kept *sucking at all the wrong times.*

14. What's the sexiest thing about Halloween? The *costumes that come off faster than candy wrappers.*

15. Why don't ghosts ever get laid? Because they can't keep their *sheets on.*

16. What's the naughtiest thing you can say at a Halloween party? "*I've got a trick you'll want to treat.*"

17. Why don't pumpkins ever hook up? Because they don't want to get *squashed.*

18. What's a zombie's favorite kind of foreplay? A little *necking.*

19. Why did the haunted house cancel its date? Because it couldn't handle the *screams of passion.*

20. What's the sexiest candy? *Jawbreakers*—for obvious reasons.

Thanksgiving Dirty Jokes

21. Why did the turkey refuse to hook up? Because it was tired of getting *stuffed every year.*

22. What's the dirtiest thing you can say at Thanksgiving dinner? *"Who wants to butter my buns?"*

23. Why did the gravy boat get jealous? Because it saw someone else *spreading the love.*

24. What's a turkey's least favorite position? *Bent over the table.*

25. Why don't mashed potatoes ever flirt? Because they're already *whipped.*

26. What's the worst thing to hear during Thanksgiving? *"This stuffing isn't the only thing that's going in tonight."*

27. Why do pies love the holidays? Because they always get to *show off their fillings.*

28. Why did the cranberry sauce get kicked out of the party? Because it was too *tart to handle.*

29. What's the dirtiest thing a turkey can say? *"Baste me, baby."*

30. Why do families fight on Thanksgiving? Because someone always *spills the beans—and their wine.*

Valentine's Day Dirty Jokes

31. Why don't Cupid's arrows ever miss? Because they're always *aimed below the belt.*

32. What's worse than a bad Valentine's gift? One that comes with the phrase, "*It's the thought that counts.*"

33. Why did the box of chocolates break up with the teddy bear? Because it wanted someone with *harder fillings.*

34. What's the sexiest Valentine's Day surprise? One that involves *handcuffs and no interruptions.*

35. Why don't roses make good lovers? Because they're *too thorny to handle.*

36. Why did the couple argue on Valentine's Day? Because someone forgot to *polish the candy heart.*

37. What's a hopeless romantic's favorite kind of kiss? One that *lasts longer than their ex.*

38. Why don't Cupid and Santa hang out? Because they're tired of *delivering for ungrateful people.*

39. What's the worst thing to hear on Valentine's Day? "*Let's talk about us.*"

40. Why do people love February 15th? Because it's all about *cheap chocolates and no commitments.*

New Year's Dirty Jokes

41. What's the worst thing to say at a New Year's party? *"I've got a resolution for both of us—and it involves less clothing."*

42. Why don't people hook up on New Year's Eve? Because no one wants to start the year with *regrets.*

43. What's a champagne bottle's favorite move? *Popping off* at the right moment.

44. Why do New Year's kisses always feel better? Because they're *full of promise and bad intentions.*

45. Why did the ball drop early? Because it couldn't handle the *pressure.*

46. What's the sexiest part of New Year's Eve? The countdown to *bad decisions.*

47. Why don't people make resolutions in bed? Because they're too busy *breaking them immediately.*

48. What's worse than a bad kiss at midnight? Realizing they're already *thinking about someone else.*

49. Why did the clock blush? Because it saw someone *losing track of time—and their pants.*

50. What's the most awkward part of New Year's Eve? Explaining why you're still single after all those *fireworks.*

Holidays will never feel the same after these jokes! Ready to take things up another notch with Random and Outrageous jokes? Let's keep the laughter (and blushing) going!

Chapter 11: Random and Outrageous – Anything Goes

Sometimes the best jokes are the ones that don't fit into a neat category—they're chaotic, unexpected, and outrageously dirty. Buckle up for these 100 completely wild and random dirty jokes that'll make you laugh, blush, and maybe question your life choices.

1. Why did the cucumber file a complaint?

Because it was tired of being *in everyone's salads.*

2. What's worse than getting caught naked?

Getting caught *with socks on.*

3. Why did the banana refuse to date the apple?

Because it couldn't handle *another peeling relationship.*

4. What's a plumber's favorite type of foreplay?

Fixing the pipes before things get messy.

5. Why don't donuts ever hook up?

Because they don't want to get *glazed and confused.*

6. What's a rooster's favorite pickup line?

"Wanna cock-a-doodle-doo me?"

7. Why did the blender get dumped?

Because it couldn't stop *spinning out of control.*

8. Why do escalators hate relationships?

Because they're always *going up and down.*

9. What's the worst thing to say during foreplay?

"Hold on, I just need to check my phone."

10. Why did the vacuum cleaner blush?

Because it saw someone *getting sucked off.*

11. Why do printers make bad lovers?

Because they're always *jammed at the wrong time.*

12. What's a stripper's least favorite type of cash?

Monopoly money.

13. Why did the ladder break up with the broom?

Because it couldn't handle all the *sweeping issues.*

14. What's a cat's favorite position?

Purring on top.

15. Why don't trees ever get into relationships?

Because they're afraid of getting *axed.*

16. Why did the ice cube break up with the whiskey?

Because it felt like it was *melting under pressure.*

17. What's the dirtiest thing you can say at a barbecue?

"Who wants to handle my meat first?"

18. Why did the clock refuse to date the calendar?

Because it didn't want to *lose time.*

19. What's a baker's favorite kind of sex?

Frosting the buns after heating things up.

20. Why did the watermelon go to therapy?

Because it felt like it was *seeding doubt* in its relationships.

21. What's a magician's favorite pickup line?

"Want me to make your clothes disappear?"

22. Why did the pepper grinder flirt with the salt shaker?

Because it wanted to *spice things up.*

23. Why do candles love romance?

Because they know how to *burn for someone.*

24. What's a fisherman's favorite position?

The *hook and release.*

25. Why do waterbeds make terrible lovers?

Because they're *always making waves* at the wrong time.

26. What's the sexiest fruit?

Peaches, because they've got the juiciest bottoms.

27. Why don't socks ever hook up?

Because they're always *looking for their perfect match.*

28. What's a surfer's favorite kind of foreplay?

Riding the waves before diving in.

29. Why did the chicken refuse to cross the road?

Because it heard someone wanted to *pluck it.*

30. What's worse than being left on read?

Being told, "*Wrong person.*"

31\. Why did the bed break up with the mattress?

Because it was tired of *carrying all the weight.*

32\. What's the most awkward thing to say during a date?

"*This feels like something I'd tell my therapist.*"

33\. Why don't forks ever flirt?

Because they don't want to *get stuck in anything messy.*

34\. What's the sexiest thing about construction workers?

The way they know how to *lay a solid foundation.*

35\. Why did the boat refuse to date the anchor?

Because it didn't want to *be held down.*

36\. What's a miner's favorite position?

The one where they get to *dig deep.*

37\. Why don't airplanes flirt?

Because they're too busy *taking off in the wrong directions.*

38\. What's a pizza's favorite move?

Getting topped in all the right places.

39\. Why don't guitars make good lovers?

Because they're always *strumming the wrong chord.*

40. What's the worst thing to hear during sex?

"*Wait, is this a bad time to talk about my ex?*"

41. Why do trampolines make bad lovers?

Because they'll *bounce on you* and never call back.

42. What's a plumber's worst nightmare?

Overflowing emotions in the wrong pipe.

43. Why don't roses make good partners?

Because they're *prickly in all the wrong places.*

44. Why did the hose get fired?

Because it couldn't stop *spraying everywhere.*

45. What's worse than a bad kiss?

One that comes with *too much tongue and no control.*

46. Why did the hot tub flirt with the swimming pool?

Because it wanted to *heat things up.*

47. What's a bread's worst fear?

Getting *toasted and forgotten.*

48. Why do elevators make the best lovers?

Because they know how to *go up and down smoothly.*

49. Why did the pillow cry?

Because it saw what happened during the *pillow fight.*

50. What's the worst thing to whisper in someone's ear?

"*Did you remember to lock the door?*"

51. Why don't plumbers ever get lonely?

Because they're always surrounded by *dirty pipes.*

52. What's the dirtiest pick-up line ever?

"Are you a washing machine? Because I'd love to throw my dirty load in you."

53. Why did the banana go to the party?

Because it wanted to *split* with someone hot.

54. What do you call a naked cow?

Udderly exposed.

55. Why did the peach blush?

Because it saw the cucumber *getting pickled.*

56. Why don't candles ever cheat?

Because they always burn for their *one true flame.*

57. Why are tacos so sexy?

Because they've got all the *right fillings.*

58. What do you call a horny electrician?

A *shock jock.*

59. Why don't eggs ever hook up?

Because they're too afraid of getting *scrambled.*

60. What's the dirtiest thing you can say to a chef?

"Let me taste your *meatballs.*"

61. Why do pirates make terrible lovers?

Because they always come *too fast.*

62. What's a magician's favorite kind of foreplay?

Disappearing acts.

63. Why did the cucumber go to therapy?

Because it couldn't handle all the *pressure.*

64. What's the most inappropriate thing you can say at a wedding?

"Does anyone object? Because I'd *totally hit that.*"

65. Why are donuts so flirty?

Because they always have a *hole lot of love to give.*

66. What's a baker's idea of foreplay?

Frosting the buns.

67. Why did the toothbrush break up with the toothpaste?

Because it couldn't handle all the *morning breath.*

68. What's the difference between a microwave and a date?

At least the microwave gets *hot in seconds.*

69. Why don't vampires use condoms?

Because they already have *immortal protection.*

70. What's the sexiest vegetable?

Corn on the cob—it's got the perfect grip.

21. Why did the vacuum cleaner get fired?

Because it was caught *sucking off the competition.*

72. What's a gym rat's favorite position?

Leg day.

73. Why do fishermen love dirty jokes?

Because they're always *casting their nets wide.*

74. Why don't roosters ever flirt?

Because they're too busy *cock-a-doodling*.

75. What's the dirtiest thing you can say in a car?

"Want me to *shift your stick?*"

76. Why did the trucker blush?

Because the GPS kept telling him to *make a U-turn.*

77. Why don't skeletons date?

Because they don't have the *bones to pick someone up.*

78. What do you call a sexy tree?

Hardwood.

79. Why do farmers make the best lovers?

Because they know how to *plow all night.*

80. Why did the pickle break up with the jar?

It needed more *space to grow.*

81. What's a firefighter's favorite position?

The *hose-down.*

82. Why do bees make great lovers?

Because they know how to *buzz you just right.*

83. What's the difference between a trampoline and a lover?

You take your shoes off before jumping on a *trampoline.*

84. Why did the pineapple get dumped?

Because it was too *prickly* in bed.

85. What's a butcher's idea of flirting?

"Let me *meat* you in private."

86. Why are trains so romantic?

Because they're always *on track*.

87. Why don't bananas need partners?

Because they come with their own *protection*.

88. What's a dog's favorite dirty joke?

Anything that involves *bone-ing*.

89. Why did the onion break up with the garlic?

Because it couldn't handle the *layers of drama*.

90. What's a skier's favorite type of foreplay?

Going downhill fast.

91. Why don't penguins cheat?

Because they're all about keeping things *ice-cold*.

92. What's a roofer's favorite position?

Over the top.

93. Why are fruits terrible in bed?

Because they're too *juicy* to handle.

94. What do you call a sexy plumber?

Someone who knows how to *lay the pipe*.

95. Why did the train conductor get fired?

Too many *inappropriate stops.*

96. Why are pizzas the best lovers?

Because they come in *all the right sizes.*

97. What's the dirtiest thing you can say in an elevator?

"Going *down*?!"

98. Why do actors make bad lovers?

Because they're always faking the *climax.*

99. What's a fisherman's favorite position?

The *catch and release.*

100. Why don't showers ever hook up?

Because they're too *clean-cut.*

Chapter 12: The Ultimate Naughty Collection – 100 Extra Spicy Jokes

This chapter is where the gloves (and filters) come off! Dive into this outrageous collection of 100 dirty and wildly inappropriate jokes that will leave you laughing, cringing, and maybe even turning a little red.

Naughty One-Liners

1. Why don't oysters donate to charity? Because they're too *shellfish...* but they sure know how to make you moan.

2. Why don't condoms ever lie? Because they're *transparent about their intentions.*

3. What's the worst thing to say after sex? *"Well, that was something."*

4. Why did the banana refuse to hook up? It didn't want to get *split in half.*

5. Why don't ghosts make good lovers? Because they can't keep their *sheets on.*

6. Why did the watermelon refuse to date the pineapple? Because it couldn't handle its *prickly personality.*

7. What's a pizza's favorite position? *Extra toppings.*

8. Why do guitars make bad partners? Because they're always *strumming someone else's strings.*

9. Why did the vacuum cleaner blush? It saw someone *getting sucked off.*

10. What's worse than bad sex? When they say, "*That's it?*"

11. Why did the snowman file for divorce? Because the snowwoman was *too cold in bed.*

12. Why don't gym rats date? Because they're all about *quick reps and no commitments.*

13. What's the difference between a drink and a date? A drink always gets you *tipsy in a good way.*

14. Why did the blender get fired? Because it couldn't stop *mixing up feelings.*

15. Why don't plumbers ever get lonely? Because they're always *laying pipe.*

16. What's worse than being ghosted? Finding out they're haunting someone else.

17. Why did the teddy bear get dumped? Because it was too *soft in the wrong places.*

18. Why did the clock blush? Because it saw the hands *going all over each other.*

19. Why don't escalators make good lovers? Because they're always *rushing up and down.*

20. Why do construction workers make great lovers? Because they know how to *build things up before tearing them down.*

Flirty and Spicy

21. Why did the chili pepper flirt with the onion? Because it wanted to *make things hot and steamy.*

22. What's the difference between love and lust? About three shots of tequila.

23. Why don't candles ever cheat? Because they *burn only for one person at a time.*

24. What's the dirtiest thing to say at dinner? "*Who wants to butter my buns?*"

25. Why did the ghost refuse to date the vampire? It didn't want to get *sucked dry.*

26. What's worse than a bad kiss? When it feels like a *wet dog is licking your face.*

27. Why don't witches date mortals? Because they can't handle the *magic in bed.*

28. Why did the ice cube break up with the whiskey? It felt like it was *melting under pressure.*

29. Why don't donuts flirt? Because they're afraid of getting *glazed and confused.*

30. What's the kinkiest thing about blankets? They know how to *wrap you up tight.*

31. Why did the skeleton break up with its partner? Because it didn't have enough *backbone.*

32. What's worse than being caught cheating? Being caught *and liking it too much.*

33. Why do surfers make great partners? Because they know how to *ride the waves of passion.*

34. Why did the boat refuse to date the anchor? It didn't want to get *weighed down.*

35. What's the dirtiest thing to say at a gym? "*Want to spot me while I squat?*"

36. Why don't beds ever lie? Because they've *seen it all.*

37. What's a lamp's favorite thing to do? Get *turned on.*

38. Why did the moon flirt with the stars? It wanted to *light up the night in all the right ways.*

39. Why don't escalators hook up? Because they're too *afraid of mixed signals.*

40. What's the worst thing to hear in bed? "*I think we need to talk.*"

Cheeky and Bold

41. Why did the chicken cross the road? To get to the *other side piece.*

42. What's the difference between an email and a kiss? At least a kiss isn't marked *spam.*

43. Why don't pillows date each other? Because they're *tired of getting fluffed up for nothing.*

44. Why do elevators make the best lovers? Because they know how to *go up and down smoothly.*

45. What's the dirtiest thing in a kitchen? The *whisk that's been whipped too many times.*

46. Why did the peach flirt with the grape? Because it wanted a little *wine and dine action.*

47. What's a miner's favorite position? *Digging deep.*

48. Why did the watermelon go to therapy? Because it felt *too seedy inside.*

49. What's a coffee cup's favorite line? "*Fill me up and let's get steamy.*"

50. Why don't chairs flirt? Because they're tired of *being sat on by everyone.*

51. Why do trains make bad partners? Because they're always *derailing plans.*

52. What's the worst thing to say after a hookup? "*So, do you want to Venmo me for this room?*"

53. Why did the fan get dumped? It was too *blow-y for anyone's taste.*

54. What's worse than a bad date? One that ends with "*This was fun, let's do it again!*"

55. Why don't frying pans date? Because they don't want to get *burned again.*

56. What's the dirtiest thing in a bedroom? The *laundry pile everyone pretends isn't there.*

57. Why do pizzas make great lovers? Because they're always *hot and ready to please.*

58. What's worse than being ghosted? Being told, "*You're just not my type.*"

59. Why do ghosts love Halloween? Because it's their chance to *get freaky in the sheets.*

60. Why did the cheese flirt with the cracker? Because it wanted to *spread a little love.*

Wild and Inappropriate

61. Why did the blender break up with the toaster? Because it couldn't handle the *heat.*

62. What's worse than bad sex? When they say, "*That was nice.*"

63. Why did the fish hook refuse to date? It didn't want to get *reeled in too quickly.*

64. Why do gym rats love mirrors? Because they're *always looking for new positions.*

65. Why did the light bulb blush? Because it saw someone *getting screwed in the socket.*

66. What's worse than a bad kiss? A *good kiss that leads nowhere.*

67. Why did the duvet dump the pillow? Because it wanted to *cover new territory.*

68. Why don't witches date? Because they're *too busy casting spells in bed.*

69. What's the kinkiest thing about yoga mats? They know how to *support all the positions.*

70. Why did the apple refuse to date the pear? Because it didn't want to get *squeezed into a juice box.*

71. What's a squirrel's favorite pickup line? "*Want me to nut on you?*"

72. Why did the paper clip get dumped? Because it was too *clingy.*

73. Why do people love tacos? Because they're *always ready to be filled.*

74. Why did the fridge get fired? Because it couldn't keep its *cool during the heat of the moment.*

75. What's worse than a one-night stand? When it's *memorable for all the wrong reasons.*

76. Why don't staplers date? Because they don't want to *be stuck with anyone.*

77. What's a hammer's favorite kind of foreplay? *Nailing the details before hitting the mark.*

The Ultimate Dirty Jokes for Adults

78. Why did the carpet blush? Because it saw what was happening *on top of it.*

79. Why do chairs love romance? Because they're *always getting carried away.*

80. What's the dirtiest thing you can say during dinner? "*Who wants to lick the spoon?*"

81. Why don't printers ever date? Because they're *too paper-thin for commitment.*

82. What's the worst thing to hear after a date? "*So, what are we?*"

83. Why do beds make the best lovers? Because they *hold you through everything.*

84. Why did the whiskey refuse to flirt? Because it didn't want to *mix emotions.*

85. What's worse than bad foreplay? Foreplay that *ends before it begins.*

86. Why did the cat flirt with the mouse? Because it wanted to *pounce on the opportunity.*

87. Why do candles love the dark? Because they can *burn brighter in private.*

88. What's a washing machine's favorite move? *The spin cycle.*

89. Why did the door lock itself? Because it wanted to keep things *private.*

90. Why did the fork get dumped? Because it was too *sharp-tongued.*

91. What's a wine bottle's favorite phrase? "*Pop me and let's get it on.*"

92. Why do mirrors love lovers? Because they get to *see all the action.*

93. What's a toaster's biggest fear? *Burning out before the bread is ready.*

94. Why do penguins make bad lovers? Because they're too *cold in the sheets.*

95. What's the dirtiest thing to say in a kitchen? "*Let's whip this up together.*"

96. Why do bananas love bedtime? Because it's their chance to *peel away the layers.*

97. What's a plumber's favorite pickup line? "*Let me fix your pipes.*"

98. Why did the balloon blush? Because it saw someone *getting blown up.*

99. Why do surfers make terrible flirts? Because they're *always riding the wrong waves.*

100. What's the sexiest thing about clouds? The way they *drift into naughty shapes.*

Chapter 13: Make Your Friends Blush – Sharing Tips and Situational Humor

Telling dirty jokes is an art form. Get it right, and you're the life of the party. Get it wrong, and you're *that person* no one wants to sit nearby. This chapter is all about delivering those spicy punchlines with finesse and confidence, so you can make your friends laugh, blush, and maybe even snort their drink out of their nose.

Tips for Sharing Dirty Jokes Like a Pro

1. Know Your Audience: Don't whip out a vibrator joke at your niece's birthday

party... unless your niece is 30 and everyone's already drunk.

2. Timing is Everything: The punchline hits harder after a *perfect pause.* Build suspense, then deliver with confidence.

3. Read the Room: If people are already laughing at mildly inappropriate jokes, crank it up. If they're clutching their pearls, maybe save the raunchier stuff for later.

4. Delivery is Key: Use facial expressions, body language, and the right tone to sell the joke. Own the awkwardness—it's part of the fun.

5. Don't Be the Repeat Offender: Keep your material fresh. No one wants to hear the same dirty pun you told last week.

Situational Dirty Jokes

Here are 50 context-based dirty jokes you can use depending on the vibe of the room.

At a Wedding:

1. "Marriage is like a deck of cards. At first, all you need are two hearts and a diamond. By the end, you're wishing for a club and a spade."

2. "Do you, [Name], promise to love, honor, and occasionally fake a headache?"

At the Office:

3. "Our office has the best teamwork. Yesterday, we all pitched in to ignore an email together."

4. "Work is like foreplay. Half the time, it's awkward, and the other half, you're just pretending to enjoy it."

At a Bar:

5. "Bartender, I'll have a drink strong enough to make me think karaoke is a good idea."

6. "Why are cocktails so flirty? Because they've got all the right moves—stirred, shaken, and poured just right."

On a Date:

7. "Are you a parking ticket? Because you've got *fine* written all over you."

8. "I'm not saying you're hot, but I might have to call the fire department before dessert."

At the Gym:

9. "Why don't treadmills ever date? Because they can't handle all the *running around.*"

10. "You must be a pull-up bar, because you're raising my standards."

At a Holiday Party:

11. "Why did Santa break up with his girlfriend? She couldn't handle his *big sack.*"

12. "The best part of New Year's Eve? Kissing someone who won't remember it in the morning."

With Friends:

13. "What's the difference between a friend and a best friend? A friend helps you move; a best friend helps you *move a body.*"

14. "You know you're close friends when you can roast each other without anyone crying… until later."

At a Family Gathering (with *very* cool relatives):

15. "Why did the turkey avoid Tinder? It was tired of being *stuffed and ghosted.*"

16. "Grandma asked why I'm still single, so I asked her why her curtains smell like mothballs. We're even."

At the Gym (again, because it's a goldmine):

17. "Why did the dumbbell get dumped? It was too *heavy-handed* in the relationship."
18. "You must be a squat rack, because I'd bend over backwards for you."

On Vacation:

19. "Why do sunbathers always flirt? Because they're *hot and bothered*."
20. "You know what they say about beach flings—they're all about *sand, sweat, and bad decisions.*"

On a Road Trip:

21. "Why did the GPS blush? Because it kept saying, 'Make a U-turn.'"
22. "Road trips are fun until someone farts and locks the windows."

At a Bachelor/Bachelorette Party:

23. "Why did the stripper refuse to dance? Because someone paid with Monopoly money."

24. "The only thing that should be harder than the drinks tonight is the groom."

At a Cookout:

25. "What's the secret to a great BBQ? *Good meat and the perfect buns.*"

26. "Why did the grill flirt with the spatula? Because it wanted to *get flipped over.*"

With Your Partner:

27. "Are we having dessert tonight? Because I'd love to eat something *sweet and sticky.*"

28. "Babe, I'm not saying I'm bad at pillow talk, but you just fell asleep mid-sentence."

Quick One-Liners for Any Situation

29. "You're not a snack. You're the whole damn buffet."

30. "I didn't come here to make friends. I came here to make *questionable decisions.*"

31. "Life's too short for bad coffee, bad sex, or bad jokes."

32. "I'm not lazy. I'm just on *energy-saving mode.*"

33. "They say money can't buy happiness, but it can buy a bottle of tequila, which is close enough."

34. "If laughter is the best medicine, this book should come with a prescription."

35. "I'm not drunk. I'm just *preparing for karaoke.*"

36. "You know you've had a good night when you wake up with a hangover and a bag of fries you don't remember ordering."

37. "I don't make mistakes. I create *learning opportunities.*"

38. "Why did the sexy lamp get dumped? Because it wasn't *turned on* anymore."

39. "If I had a dollar for every bad decision I've made, I'd still spend it all on tacos."

40. "Why don't we ever take life too seriously? Because we're all just here for the *laughs and cocktails.*"

Chapter 14: Bonus Section – Extra Dirty Gems

Because we all need a little extra spice in our lives, here's a collection of jokes that didn't fit into any single category but are guaranteed to have you rolling on the floor—or running for cover. These are the unapologetically outrageous, boundary-pushing jokes you'll want to share with your wildest friends.

The Top 50 Extra Dirty Gems

1. Why don't oysters donate to charity? Because they're a little *shellfish*—but they'll still make you moan.

2. What's the sexiest part of a pencil?
   The eraser—it always gives you a *second chance*.

3. Why do men love big TVs?
   Because they can't handle *complex relationships* like small remotes.

4. Why did the cucumber call in sick?
   It couldn't handle the pressure of being *stuck in everyone's salads.*

5. What's the difference between a pizza and a partner?
   A pizza never complains about how you eat it.

6. Why don't pirates make great lovers?
   They're always *plundering the booty* too quickly.

7. What's the difference between me and a mosquito?
   A mosquito knows when to stop *sucking.*

8. Why did the vibrator get invited to the party?
   Because it knows how to *keep things buzzing.*

9. What do you call a bed with bad intentions?
   A *spring-loaded trap.*

10. Why did the blanket start flirting?
    It wanted someone to *cover up with.*

Foodie Fun

11. Why don't vegetables ever hook up? Because they can't handle being *steamed.*

12. What's the dirtiest thing you can say at dinner?
"*Pass the meat, but hold the sausage.*"

13. Why did the whipped cream get fired? Because it kept getting *on top of everything.*

14. What's a banana's favorite move in bed? The *peel-and-reveal.*

15. Why did the bread blush? Because it saw someone *buttering up its buns.*

Animal Antics

16. Why are cows such flirts? Because they always *milk the attention.*

17. Why don't pigs ever date? Because they hate getting *roasted* about their size.

18. Why are cats so sexy? Because they know how to *get on top and make you purr.*

19. Why do chickens hate commitment?
    They don't want to *put all their eggs in one basket.*

20. What do you call a horny goat?
    A *baaa-d idea.*

Bathroom Humor

21. Why did the toilet paper break up with the roll?
    It got tired of being *wiped out.*

22. Why don't sinks ever flirt?
    Because they're afraid of getting *drained.*

23. Why did the plumber blush?
    Because they saw too many *exposed pipes.*

24. What's the sexiest thing about a bathroom mirror?
    It sees you *when you're wet.*

25. Why did the shower refuse to date?
    It couldn't handle all the *dirty talk.*

Bedroom Bloopers

26. Why do beds hate one-night stands?
    Because they never get any *sleep.*

27. Why did the lingerie feel awkward?
    Because it couldn't *cover up its feelings.*

28. What's the dirtiest thing you can say to your partner?
 "I forgot to do the laundry, so it's just us and the couch."

29. Why did the mattress feel embarrassed?
 Because it got caught *springing into action.*

30. Why are headboards so noisy?
 Because they can't *handle the banging.*

Random Outrageous Gems

31. Why don't escalators make good lovers?
 Because they're always *moving too fast.*

32. Why do laptops make terrible partners?
 Because they're *hot* for everyone.

33. What's the sexiest type of construction?
 Laying the foundation... brick by brick.

34. Why do cameras make bad lovers?
 Because they're always *focusing on someone else.*

35. Why are airports so romantic?
 Because everyone's trying to make a *connection.*

36. Why did the hot tub start dating the swimming pool?
 Because it wanted someone who could handle *deep feelings.*

37. Why do elevators make the worst dates? Because they always *let you down.*

38. Why don't staplers ever hook up? They're afraid of getting *stuck.*

39. Why are candles the best lovers? Because they're always *burning with passion.*

40. Why do printers get so frustrated? Because they can't handle too many *hard copies.*

Quick and Dirty One-Liners

41. "I'm not lazy, I'm just *recharging for later.*"

42. "What's my favorite position? Any position where I don't have to move."

43. "My love life is like Wi-Fi: *connected in public, disconnected at home.*"

44. "If my bed could talk, it'd probably just ask for a break."

45. "What's the sexiest drink? *Anything strong enough to lower my standards.*"

46. "Why don't I date gym buffs? Because I like someone with *soft abs and strong opinions.*"

47. "Why are tacos better than relationships? Because they don't leave you *crying after three bites.*"

48. "What's the difference between me and a pizza? A pizza gets *topped more often.*"

49. "Why do I love tequila? Because it erases *my regrets and my boundaries.*"

50. "If laughter is the best medicine, this book is the *pharmacy of filth.*"

Acknowledgments: To the Real Dirty Minds Behind the Laughs

Writing this book was no small feat—it took guts, giggles, and just the right amount of inappropriate inspiration. So, let's take a moment to give a big shoutout to all the people, places, and situations that made this masterpiece possible.

To My Friends and Family

Thanks for putting up with my terrible jokes at every dinner, party, and awkward family gathering. You might never look at me the same way again, but hey, you knew what you were signing up for.

To My Coworkers

For tolerating my endless barrage of inappropriate office humor. I promise I'll stop photocopying jokes and leaving them on the copier... maybe.

To Every Awkward Date I've Ever Had

You taught me that humor is the best way to survive the cringe-worthy silences—and sometimes the only way to escape the bill.

To Bartenders Everywhere

For laughing at my terrible pickup lines and not kicking me out when I asked if your cocktail shaker ever gets tired of all the *shaking.*

To the Internet

Because let's face it, without memes, dirty puns, and endless inspiration, this book wouldn't exist. Thanks for keeping it spicy, random, and just inappropriate enough.

And Finally, To You

The brave, wonderful, possibly unhinged person reading this book. Thank you for embracing the chaos, the filth, and the laughter. Whether you're reading this alone, sharing it with friends, or whispering these jokes to your partner in bed (you cheeky devil), you're the real MVP.

Now, if you're not blushing or rolling your eyes, then I haven't done my job. But if you laughed out loud—or snorted your drink at least once—then we're officially best friends now. Let's hang out again soon.

Conclusion: Keep Laughing, Keep Living

Humor is what keeps life interesting, and dirty jokes? Well, they're the spice that makes the bland moments a little tastier. If this book taught you anything, it's that laughter is the ultimate icebreaker, the best cure for awkwardness, and sometimes, the only thing standing between you and total chaos.

So, here's my advice:

- Tell these jokes with confidence.
- Share them responsibly (or irresponsibly, we're not judging).

- And never stop looking for the humor in life's messiest moments.

Remember: a good dirty joke doesn't just make people laugh—it brings them closer. So go out there, tell some wildly inappropriate jokes, and make the world a little brighter… or at least a little weirder.

Cheers to living, laughing, and never taking anything too seriously. Until next time!

Your Turn to Shine! Got a dirty joke that didn't make it into the book? Share it with me on social media (IG or FB) David Moo Official or at www.davidmoo.co.uk. Who knows—you might just inspire the next edition.

Would you do me a favor?

If you enjoyed reading this book, would you be nice enough to write a review on the platform you got it from?

Or maybe you could recommend this book on your social media to your friends and family?

Trust me, it literally takes less than a minute but it goes a long way to help our very small publishing business.

All the Best xX

Victor :)

Made in the USA
Las Vegas, NV
01 April 2025